Yellow Umbrella Books are published by Red Brick Learning
7825 Telegraph Road, Bloomington, Minnesota 55438
http://www.redbricklearning.com

Library of Congress Cataloging-in-Publication Data
Ring, Susan.
    [Big or small? Spanish and English]
    Big or small?/by Susan Ring = ¿Grande o chiquito?/por Susan Ring.
    p. cm.
    Summary: "Simple text and photos show that animals can be big or small and can
be sorted into groups by their size"—Provided by publisher.
    Includes index.
    ISBN-13: 978-0-7368-6019-2 (hardcover)
    ISBN-10: 0-7368-6019-3 (hardcover)
    1. Proportion—Juvenile literature. 2. Size perception—Juvenile literature. I. Title:
¿Grande o chiquito? II. Title.
QA117.R5618 2006
152.14'2—dc22   2005025850

Written by Susan Ring
Developed by Raindrop Publishing

Editorial Director: Mary Lindeen
Editor: Jennifer Van Voorst
Photo Researcher: Wanda Winch
Adapted Translations: Gloria Ramos
Spanish Language Consultants: Jesús Cervantes, Anita Constantino
Conversion Assistants: Jenny Marks, Laura Manthe

Photo Credits
Cover: Grant Woodrow/Image Ideas, Inc; Title Page: Photo 24/Brand X Pictures;
Page 4: Deirdre Barton/Capstone Press; Page 6: Deirdre Barton/Capstone Press;
Page 8: Richard T. Nowitz/Corbis; Page 10: Bill Hilton Jr./Hilton Pond Center;
Page 12: David Pinquoch/Alaska Good Time Charters; Page 14: Melissa Rickers/
USDA Forest Service/Chippewa National Forest; Page 16: Ralf Schmode

1 2 3 4 5 6 11 10 09 08 07 06

Big or Small?
by Susan Ring

¿Grande o chiquito?
por Susan Ring

Yellow
Umbrella
Books
for early readers

4

This horse is big.

Este caballo es grande.

This horse is small.

Este caballo es chiquito.

This bird is big.

Este pájaro es grande.

This bird is small.

Este pájaro es chiquito.

This fish is big.

Este pez es grande.

This fish is small.

Este pez es chiquito.

Who is big?
Who is small?

¿Quién es grande?
¿Quién es chiquito?

Index

Índice